The Departure

CHRIS EMERY lives in Cromer with his wife and children. He works in publishing. His has written two previous collections of poetry, a writer's guide and edited editions of Emily Brontë, John Keats and Christina Rossetti. His work has been widely published in magazines and anthologised, most recently in *Identity Parade: New British and Irish Poets* (Bloodaxe, 2010). He is a contributor to *The Cambridge Companion to Creative Writing* (Cambridge University Press, 2012), edited by David Morley and Philip Neilsen.

Also by Chris Emery

POETRY
Dr. Mephisto
Radio Nostalgia
The Departure

CHAPBOOKS
The Cutting Room

WRITERS' GUIDES
101 Ways to Make Poems Sell: The Salt Guide to Getting and Staying Published

AS EDITOR
Poets in View: A Visual Anthology of 50 Classic Poems
Emily Brontë: The Visionary and Other Poems
John Keats: Ode to Psyche and Other Poems
Christina Rossetti: Goblin Market and Other Poems

AS CONTRIBUTOR
The Cambridge Companion to Creative Writing,
edited by David Morley and Philip Neilsen
The Insiders' Guide to Independent Publishing,
edited by the Independent Publishers Guild
The Writer's Handbook, edited by Barry Turner

The Departure

by

CHRIS EMERY

SALT

LONDON

PUBLISHED BY SALT PUBLISHING
12 Norwich Road, Cromer, Norfolk NR27 0AX, United Kingdom

First edition published 2012
Second edition 2015

Printed and bound in the United Kingdom by Lightning Source UK Ltd

Typeset in Paperback 9 / 13

ISBN 978 1 907773 15 0 hardback
ISBN 978 1 78643 073 7 paperback

1 3 5 7 9 8 6 4 2

for my family

Contents

Acknowledgements

The author is grateful to the editors of the following publications, in which some of these poems, often in earlier versions, first appeared: the *Guardian, Ink Sweat & Tears, Magma, The Manhattan Review, PN Review, Poetry Wales, Eleutheria – The Scottish Poetry Review*.

'Carl's Job' and 'The Destroyers' Convention' appeared in *Identity Parade: New British and Irish Poets* (Bloodaxe 2010). 'Guest Starring' is anthologised in *Split Screen* (Red Squirrel Press, 2012) edited by Andy Jackson.

I'm especially grateful to Ian Duhig, John Kinsella, Rob A. Mackenzie, David Morley, George Szirtes and Tony Williams for their generous advice with the book.

I would also like to thank my editor at Salt, Roddy Lumsden, for bringing me into the fold.

The Departure

"This morning I am ready if you are,
To hear you speaking in your new language."

– 'A Note to the Difficult One', W. S. GRAHAM

.

Snails

Snails are death's pale eccentrics. They are the lethargy
every husband chews on in his sleep, biting his cheeks.
You can fit one thousand of their tiny mouths beneath your eyelid.

They spend their bloodless nights mouthing the word 'oracle'
beside the fuming pumps. Outlets gargle with their grey supper.
Why are they all called Tony or Erasmus or King Nacre?

Tonight they will extinguish all the red dresses in the world,
then weigh out the bones of your ears
and pile them into wigwams in the dirt.

They keep trying to form this mighty ending
that hangs, damp and frazzled, above the velvet seats
in all the garden cinemas – except they never end.

They are slowly weighing up the cruises of the children now.
Their appearance is like a secret circus act that doesn't stop.
They break into all the graves beneath the peonies and salsify.

Tonight, we will pile them, pile everything of them
into the whorl of a bucket and then we will fill it
to the top with forest tears and let the silence do its work.

On the Making of Entrances

I

No one believes anything. The carmine institute is empty.
Last night's mistakes make you weary of the climate.
This art makes so much less of us. We are forge smoke.
It isn't clear we're there yet. Later, water drubs the panes.

II

Whichever shadows make today, we smell the old crimes.
Look left, a cobbled lane and a crypt of hats.
Look right, the quartermaster is eating mutton pie.
Someone runs this way and that, berserk by the tavern.

III

Gutters improve the dateless soliloquy. *Where are the whores?*
The king is all sequins and arteries: a week of wigs, a week of pigs.
We discover the end of the universe. Our buckles rust.
History is what one hears as the elms pray. No one sings.

IV

We wash in a caul of candlelight as stars upend this earth.
Would you imagine it could occur in a bed like this?
Someone resorts to the general mist for assistance.
In the horse masks of the city, we descend the mica stairs.

The Departure

I want to tell you of the underground snow
where half art is pulled from dreams, from lungs of sorrow.
Not a black art, mind, it's beautiful as a garden, or birds on the wing,
and here each upturned moon relates its winds, its times,
though blind to the beginning as to the end. I want to tell you about
a small life lived in ordinary boredoms, occasionally yielding –
a perpendicular life measured in poor assaults on the mind,
measured in raptures and deceits, in the error-driven shout,
the multiplicities of place, where the hind
of art is coupling in the desiccated night. Safe.
It is a birthing place, not a pool of warm air shifting,
but a perpetual accident of light,
there's no done thing there, nothing especially kept,
no second sight, no registered imperfection of any kind
to escape from, it is like a cobalt mirror in which
your lips move over heaven; you might not take to heaven,
less to blessings, but this place is, even now,
resting from the colossal destroyer, to save everyone.
In its moment, which is always now and now and now, you come
to see the world's messy edges devoid of calculation,
science and perfection.

You come to trust the misjudgments beside a fire
where the midnight combs prove the brain
is a proper tankard, not for pouring or storing in the cupboard,
but a miraculous pewter world opening forever
in a limitless, truly limitless space. My heaven
is often empty and disturbing, even while the common
weather can bend the plum trees flat, or your music and telly

thump out distractions, and we lose ourselves in such things:
I want you to see this place as utterly yours, a waste-
determined leisure. Sometimes it is a punishment, too,
I'll not lie about that. You can imagine a long shot on a dolly
riding over pummelled streets where the park lights fracture
and the camera pulls up, over the loyally locked fields and brings
with it family memories boiled over, flung apart
around this damaged earth, and that camera becomes yours now,
hands us its society while it changes into memory.

All art is loss. The least of it a burial. Our charge
is to cherish the risen extent of it, like a small child
amid the shattered avenue with their wires and debris.
In this place of underground snow,
down here in the bending neighbourhood, I want you to take
the hare's hand, take the burnt road south,
find the breath's loving glare, hear lung tremor –
its whoosh and veering – know with all your body
and your mind, that in this place you are a future,
you are the boundary of a mouth. Keep crossing.
Keep on crossing there. Leave this place.
Wave to me from the other side before you turn your face.

The Gathering

You know when the world grinds its iron glove
and the town's chipped teeth shine along the rivulets
beside those corny mansions you mentioned
and everyone piles into
their minds for a while, behaving.

Where the cats wallop through the buckets
of streets and dogs unfold tongues
into displays of dusk
and you can see thin suns mainly
sinking with decisions over prisons.

It's where the grey fields show our torn insane
withered in white. It's where the trains
come flaming through under the brassieres
of old offices and Jupiter listens in,
its rusty ears, bangled, burgled.

We can meet there to smoke
our taken thoughts in the evening cupboards.
There will be opera and stars.
No one will cough or throw bolts
along the canal. Knives will be wet with meat, alone.

In the briars, we mope among plastic sheets
wavering with hairdos like a canteen.
Everyone will come. The vicar
will shake out gunmetal gowns
beside a small lake of trolleys. You will be missed.

Lake Watching

for Tadashi Okabe

I am sitting before the red weeds, Dr Tanabe,
the water is purplish, not good, not bountiful in humour or blood.
This evening's draught of mosquitoes

pepper me as they pepper 1947 *en Afrique.*
No one watches me with a pair of Rodenstocks, eating tripe.
No one is about to come, perched oddly, half-heartedly leaning on
    a hoe.

There is no thin boat on a fuming lake.
It is not a scene for exhilaration or serving whisky sours.
The stifling glade is not especially forthcoming

with lewd rapture, not in any degree, even boorish nightmare.
Age, among its simple sutures, has not brought wisdom,
nor second sight. Nor indecent memory.

I'm sitting in the red weeds, Doctor, and all I fear I can contain
is lost. Is it that we can house no special moments
while being eaten or burned by the monster?

The birds are pure-throated and bitter in their skirmishes.
The waters are not lapping. The bees are dull.
The world's industrial creatures sleep ill on other shores.

Dandelions

I like your plainness in the gravel, tucked sideways
in the manky cracks you look like a dishcloth
flattened in those corners where the pointing has come out.

You don't resist, but still endure along the sagging rec.
You're often sat next to a dog turd with lots of beetles caring.
Everything is forlorn in your colourless zone.

Take all those small relinquishments at your unnoticed day rate.
Suddenly, you are there, reminding us of seeping middle age,
going to seed in some midsummer miners' estate

with no friends or music. Perhaps you are this militant scum?
The bits we don't need beneath the sun,
somehow wielding a fantastic ordinary face.

You never go away. When I spot you being flagrant
I am usually emerging from a colossal boredom into
buoyant and extraneous ideas. You are meant to be

the perfect emblem of the wasted. Your gift
is being extra. When you brighten at dusk,
spotting the panicking social scrub

under eight floors of life tapestry,
we hear your prayers: *'Given up but still here'* and
'You get up, you get on with it', which is nearly likely, really.

Carl's Job

'We need you to cope with all the *little* jobs,' smiled Carl.
'We want to make sure you target single losers, too.'
'*Sure,*' I laughed. '*I was very sad to hear about Verna.*'
'How the hell do you know about my wife?' asked Carl.

'*I was the one who ran over her that time,*' I replied.
'You mean that time at Hennessy's; the time she died?' said Carl.
'*Right,*' I said. '*The time she died; running off of the verge.
She kept her left leg twisting. It was a little strange.*' I smiled.

'What the hell do you want with me?' asked Carl.
'*I've come to apply.*' I said. '*I want to work with you now.*'
'You want to work *with* me? I'm speechless. What do
you want to do, kill me in a wreck, maybe?' said Carl.

'*I've no further plans on killing,*' I said. '*Those days are done.*'
'Let me tell you, Bud,' said Carl. 'Those days are sitting here now.'
'*Your daughters are safe from me,*' I said. '*Your son, too.*'
'How do you know about my kids?' asked Carl. 'What is this?'

'*There's no risk here.*' I said. '*No risk at all. No graves or anything.*'
'Who mentioned graves?' said Carl. 'I don't know about no graves.'
'*This was part of my general assistance,*' I added, scraping a boot.
'Assistance?' said Carl. 'Get the hell out of here, you freak.'

'*I can't do that,*' I said. '*To my mind, things need traversing here.*'
'What kind of things are we talking about?' asked Carl.
'*Once a month,*' I said. '*I come and clean the place down. That's it.*'
'Just the lounge and shit? Nothing with the boys on the door?' asked
   Carl.

'*Just that.*' I said. '*Once a month. Though I want to bake, too.*' I said.
'What kind of baking are we speaking of here?' asked Carl.
'*I'll turn up with some gram flour and ghee, a little chicken,
some kalonji seeds and I'll cook up fresh pakora.*' I said. '*Every day.*'

'Forget it,' said Carl. 'We advertised this as a one-time loser's job.'
'*Yes,*' I agreed. '*I am right for this. No pressure here. No acid nights.*'
'Please,' said Carl. 'I can't take this from you. I lost my wife already.'
'*The pain'll cease,*' I said. '*Tomorrow I'll begin. Let's open up at five.*'

The Destroyers' Convention

All day the destroyers have arrived
handing in their burnt umbrellas to the coat check boy.
His acne shimmers above the escritoire.

He constantly derides the hotel's silver service
and the baked Alaska, the indolent chicken supreme.
Yet these ones pouring past him with abandon

squander menus like the Raj.
For hours, inside the bar, their ideal urgency swarms
below a surfeit of monocles and moustaches.

They are ravening with the history of leather,
entire family kills, evenings of Domestos.
And then their bulbous taxies draw away

into streets of amber gas.
Alighting at the Gaumont, the vetches
of the establishment watch from the gold vestibule

as the audience are reeled in over velvet and gold
to stare at the screen's foaming reservoirs,
terraces and offices, top brass,

where twill and brogues eats up
a life of hats – wholly whirring up.
Later they drink pink gins in fixed abysmal light,

their whiskers rouged. They are simple dented dolls
discussing lime kilns on their circuit
of oblivion.

Is it all so pointless, loose in pit smoke?
The gabardine life catering for
bomb blasts and mice.

On Leaving Wale Obelisk

for Jen

Did we shuck our suits that leaf-dense noon,
leaving serious careers in lemon light?
The high clouds, early swallows, the day moon
weakened, nothing farmed, nothing tight

above the summer marriage of grasses,
and all that luscious time receding in
the corporate years' climbing excesses,
just a vacancy before the children?

We made our love pledge there. It leaves you
in chromatic episodes like this,
doesn't it? Not quite nostalgia, but who
could have imagined ageing like this?

We had climbed up to lie on the piled hay,
the tow-coloured earth all nice and neat
and with everything to come our way,
lovers of the smashed-up wheat.

Duke Bluebeard

Each morning he coughs up entire corridors
of detainees.
The saturated ceilings bulge, the ball lights wobble
in each beige apartment.

This morning, he wanders out warning
the twelfth storey rays.
Knocking on doors,
tapping the struts and laths,

testing the slop on the floors with a block-toed foot:
he never wears galoshes. He is
connecting the impressive lips of the world.
He readies himself for the day's accountancy.

When Judith comes to clean the tower
she is permanently bent into the letter *R*,
ripping up piles of scarlet tulle,
picking up bran-coloured skirts, fans, court shoes, masks.

She hates his beard and throbbing *basso profondo*.
She calls him a fat goat. He tugs his beard and asks
her to open any door, this way or that. She's had it with him.
She keeps her head down.

He shrugs his shoulders and walks off boasting to the dead.
There's always tomorrow.
More floors. More doors. More ticking frames.
This world will never tire of locking up its women.

Rita's Creatures

Donny Scues' *waz-mobile* was only
heard in Mulbrox, like, several rust jobs deep,
whacking out The Cool Kids for Compton or Big D

or cruising Aldo's for a big widow glamour night.
Alien detox. *Crustadelic.* All over soil fanatics.
It made me barf. Sissy's kids were through with Greta anyways

but comforting though she was I really doubt
the seamless crotch was so fantastic in the seat.
You know it, too. That place is dog perfect.

How come eating cuties is so bad anyhow.
Gricedale's everlasting crudités always
left me smelling like clam soda or kelp and gave me gas,

like I'd done a week in Tina's salon as she poked out
one thousand L&Ms next to the extreme nail dipper.
All that chicken gone to waste.

Slow season. Big learning, burning earth day.
Some commotion held our attention for an hour
like anti-saucer vigilantes moaning about hell

as the deli off takes sashayed through Montgomery
on a featureless pine hunt, the parrots braying.
Bettie crawled out to ask, *'Is that you, Vernon?'*

The Interrogation

Several concave children gave evidence
about internal heating deficiencies, ghosts, they said,
even when the next farm was 'kiss-my-ass' Republican

it would consist of 'abominable behaviours' though
we knew parenting was edible pulp.
Anyway, Lucy's relatives were all cholesterol.

Boiling was never a precise art, not like
having hives and the itching would not subside
for days. 'Creaking is leaking,' the factor said.

For now, make contact with low-ceilinged
housing units and use the yellow jersey
sweater Maud brought from Saffron's,

the 'turkey-handed waster', as we knew her.
Powering up the certain suit was all cluster
and bluster. No one packed it in. No one moved.

Several planes coalesced into a single black basin,
pin columns, bronze integument failed to support
the listless creepers. Motion sickness everywhere,

even the loyal hangers-on seemed biting and thick.
No synapse provided proof but the buttresses
left the cellar housing all wishy washy. 'It was like a pit

of fat. We knew they were in the oil. He was a loafer, too.
Never coming out.' The desk sergeant made calls:
one with a giant gland and uppity manoeuvres

which held the bones of the family together.
The other, long distance, was less secure, 'I can break him,'
The man said. 'He will cry with the teeth of it.'

Southwold

'The Girl from Ipanema' floats out
from the Sole Bay Inn as we take note
of the ash-grey granite
of the two-up two-down opposite.
It has a charcoal push bike
leaning on the door's black velour.
The grocer's swells with fruit;
the brewery sports its brands
with a tame gold veneer.

The lighthouse pokes its tibia
into the sloe-blue night,
fathoming out the sea's soft rushes.
We hear the darker pebbles
with their foam hems, faintly clacking
their blind buds together.
All these comings and goings
where the beach's groynes order
the waves' chemical procession.

Our landlady's pensive as a courtesan.
She reads the papers in the empty lounge.
Her mornings 're scooped out between regulars.
Her red jowls mark out
the egg and tomatoes of each sallow breakfast.
All for the taking. The perfect scallops
of roof tiles on beach huts, painted like teeth.
The slow sedans in this temporary commune.

Now starlings in pyrotechnic, half-baked flight
swoop to eaves sharpened with gorgeous,
apostolic light. So much to claim,
as the sea's womb bursts and adopts
one column of light
from an aching corn-yellow moon.
We're spruced up, mediators in an evening
swollen free from cities, chalking up meaning
below the swashes of power lines.

Remember this weather. Summers silted up
like the vanguard of some redemption.
Just pan left and take a wide angle
as the score changes and we change reels.
Now that swollen moon drops and kicks up
a class finale. The brass dampened, throbbing,
as the strings come swooping in with
Fred and Ginger, dancing the perfect closing steps.

Sunday Fathers

You can almost see them there now,
the Sunday fathers, wasting time
by the swings. They seem standoffish
beneath the oaks. They've come to act

awkward at the edge of the bells
that normally invert the town,
going on from all the exits
of those roomless marriages, out

into the park's bent congregation,
testing the equipment.
It might be pouring: a morning's
upended sunlight still

beside the napped flint of some church
half boarded, closed now. The weather
is getting serious, clouds loaf
over a grudge match – you can hear

each goal in the vernacular
afternoon. We should be there with
the old boys singing or shouting,
but we deserve this world of dads,

kept out in the ordinary
almost entire absence of it.
The love lessons reversed into.
All those photographs minus one.

Everyone's pockets have loosened.
Those who survive this should get a
badge or something. This is the world
of the fewer together. The

world of bald larks and pitch and putt,
the flicks and the zoo. The world with sod all
else to do and more time for it.
Carted back for a week of fresh

earnings and maths, the children walk
from car to car, waving away
the chemistry of the endings
that recur here, artlessly.

The New Play at The Astoria

I'm watching the Baltic light decline by slow degrees.
Stage left, a gold pagoda, behind it a starry lake reduced
in the sumptuous evening. Now, the leads, in masks, isolate
their rich emotions inside the crowd, working.

Our interest lies with the bodies of the women, though,
who, while impressively restricted, are imagining their gloves.
There is a charmingly repetitive soundtrack off stage.
Beside this, the weathered temple script leads off

to tiny birds. Underneath, things develop.
At first the implications of each soft movement
seem wondrously vague, but soon the changes in our scarlet
backdrop seem peculiarly prescient, and we are enabled

to see a remote undressed yearning grove. We can't stand it.
We begin itching. Some of us are fevered enough to break loose.
The protagonists are undeterred and begin slowly waving back.
Each of us is placed into a separate fog. This is how it begins.

The Goose Moon

What are we doing above the poor sea?
Do we dream this bridge of wind
will reach the sour pines of Europe?
Why bother pouring such weather
under the goose moon.

Why bring this denying wing down
from all the worst clocks of the night
to reach no eye, no ear, no lovely wake
of punching sea and chance our white flame
in the hall-less journey here.

Why were we with the ghost snows
so far in the north, in this empty mind
where air peels and pours
in its saintless interior.

And worn out with Jupiter,
beneath our night coal, tip to tip,
we send those scouring messages
for the fat path home, queens of mint air,
and the world turns its coarse trim with us
and we are the Christmas sisters
and make the turn and the lit-up tide steers us
below the goose moon.

No one is free of the feather dream
and the polished waters ride us
all wing whisper, when the call comes to turn,
to break and lead, to return one to another

in the European night
uncovering the jarring saviours
and we imagine what is human,
unmined and working,
warm with all the land's resistance,
delivered in their houses, in taxes,
in the deaf blood of the roads below.

No. 1 Cowboy Song

Ol' gray noon roosts among the wreckage, we are a landscape
and we come through it for it ain't through with us either,

skirting meaty acres, the years cleared, I see this Choice.
Lord, this can't be how life assigns us, leavened in a lizard stand-off,

tipping us under ropey shade, for these are our young days:
like god's eagle view of earth working through its furry luggage,

and yes we're here, attending to some hound's tooth moon and its
    guitar,
us sweetly in the April redbuds and mesquite like a bent horn.

Ain't no association of cool banns, like we met in some lovers' shindig,
which was where ourselves married and the world came next, singing.

Shimmy on over, let me see your own frame in the white gospel
of heat, your rare shoulders in a demesne, everything revealed like
    a steer,

this boiling noon's shaking loose its crummy voluptuousness,
we ain't fixing to adhere to no bony treatise. No, my sweet,

we ain't fixing to adhere to penury and beans, no farm future,
no life to come but dodging fleas. We'll take horse spit every time.

Shrimpies

We're in a beach mansion for the thirty-fifth take
and I'm saddled with this pair, standing in for Tyro.
Clarissa bends and straightens to take out that kink
in her back while I'm this 'pulmonary oedema'
draped over a granite bath, taking it in
while Tyro is educating the newbies in the den.

Now Wes slides out of his wife, taking a toot,
getting loaded, going up into his 'place of nectar'.

Boulevard light spills over pink plaster
while some hard-act lifers from up-state
watch Trixie send her toys back to Alberta.
That stipple always shows on camera,
which is where my life fits in: bubble butt,
chewing sofa stains, doubling for creeps.

Mostly, I stare at tan fabrics and zebra hide,
chrome sides, cold tiling, celandine and surf.

Danny's back with tons of lube and Vinny
is at pains to provoke some 'real fucking damage'.
Coke and Viagra, margaritas, Malboros,
cans of Red Stripe, take their toll.
Whatever journeys lead here,
none reach the same place twice.

I spot the mirror tiles and think to dial home:
'Put the oven on, Hon. I'll be back in time for shrimpies.'

On Great Endings

M. drew on his theories something like this:
a cockerel springs from night brains; after breakfast
it invents Czechoslovakia amid the nodding choughs.
All the forks, the platters, the cruet set: everything is dancing.
There's no end to all the shooting in the snow.

M. is alone, it is a dishevelled evening: we turn our collars
and chase our thumbs across a desiccated fox fur,
then we reach up to pick our bloody ears.
All those lilies in the rude apartment! No one cared.
We end up married in this land of hair.

M. discards his white money and turns perpetual.
We see coarse diners fleeing, a thousand moths pour
from the chef as he leans across this green terrine.
Every plate is greasy with stew. You lead the way up
to the tired ovens. That was an entirely different ending.

M. says new lovers are just the X-Rays of a cowardice.
At 5 o'clock, we watch the coalmen jumping
in the gold bushes. M. wore his purple trunks again.
He brushed out his hair with macassar oil.
Time is the end of this Orient rope and here the night dives.

M. grew worse. He began to plug in to new strophes:
the earth's fat axles, the gunning love moons.
He swapped this tale for a silver balustrade and meant it.
Afterwards, we all wobbled down to the pier head
and into the very end of the ambrotype.

Theology

This god is chicken guts with boneless wings
chopping up buckets of sand forever.

Her skin's Elastoplast-coloured and sort of saggy.
Her eyes look like offal in a Pyrex dish.

Her beak's always clucking over those red fields of souls.
She wears Alcan all the time.

Sometimes she dances with wobbly tattooed legs
and she reads Tolkien absolutely loads.

She wears tons of bangles on her ankles
and has a guitar. The guitar has no strings though.

She is all over us like universal manure and carved angels
drop out of her bum. God is really not much good for you,

she makes up stuff she hates and closes her eyes to it
and will do you in and her priests will make you have sex a lot

and turn your head into Plasticine and squish it up.
This is a special punishment she has for bloody useless children.

We are made in the shape of god's shoes, she walks in us.
Everything is indispensable for god. Even meat shadows.

My love for her takes the form of an intricately-carved
piece of polystyrene I got, covered with soap and decals

from the god shop. There are other ones you can buy there, too,
wrapped up in tiny tie-dye dresses with faces like Rod Stewart

or Elgar. They don't have much fur. Most have no bulbs in them.
But mine is chicken guts. She is coming for you.

Each time you go past KFC you can hear god sizzling
with all these crumbs in the bubbles of creation.

M1 3LA

Up the pissy steps we find nostalgia's vein-blue glamour
sweeping under chandeliers and a dominating
stairwell, cloistered bridges and gantries
and dark batik where hoteliers in sulking combat sit.
Maybe they're fed up faking it with crimplene
for mauve itinerant weddings, or watching
the unhitched come past name-boarded rooms
straight from the sales circuit to some daft do
on sill linings or Mitsubishi extractor fans –
all scooting in from Bromley and Burnley
on £20k contracts with options for export.

The car park is all sun-roofed Mondeos.
The cladded bars are putty coloured and flooded
with Sky Sports where youth's peeling edge embarks
on suited years of margins, on the way to a dad's
divorce or dividends, drizzle and Droylsden's
best kept secret, moored to all those structured terms.

We sidle up among the winding men intent on
feeding this necrosis of signage and pull up
a pew to spot a few lame souls reading
the monthlies in Edwardian kitsch. So
gone up in the world and yet gone off. The tide
has turned, the boats have sailed and all of us
are stranded in this little local absence, making from it
what we can, not filled with laughs or money, carried
over six pints of Boddies and a go at the vids
before the bells call time and Sugsy coughs up
on the cards and Darren shuts up shop on his Chinese

bonded plastics tale; he's almost bagged it now.
Our lives are made between such repetition,
like the Manchester-Hollywood boudoir thing,
where ideas still die among the lazy girls
and rooms of cheap cutlery. Bed time now.

The salad bars are gaping still in stolidly lit suites.
Six flights up we separate into our cares like fish,
along the corridors' empty lungs in our exit
from home. We hit the fungus-shaped bed
in yeasty air and muzak, the telly freeze-framed
on a grinning line of chefs, shot in some
spittoon-shaped atrium in Gatley.

How many of us strip before the atrocity of the mirror?
Unpeeling selves like a bridge into some white error
of arse and thighs, the tide mark of pubic hair greying now.
The air con whistles and shifts its haunches. The toilet groans.
Sleepless at three, we draw back jacquard curtains
on the soaking brick Elysium, all eyes up
for what refocuses on icy city panes, those body smears
catching vacant light like a Vaseline ghost and in
those whorls we see the mad swifts' shrieking circuits
echoed over torpid crowds and feel, or half sense,
each torso lifting in the livid air, towards a trace-setting
where hopes perpetually pour.

The Canal

for Lee Rourke

Most of us end up here with a little wound
in the medical congregation
and what makes worlds of work towers up
from green chenille hems like this.
A few look on to see what's wasted,
who's in deep or who's gone wrong.

What they see's a tonne of water
gnawing at a tasselled grid, a barking dog
no light returns to, lolling vacant, round the bend.
Yet light crams in these endings now:
spare bones in black soup, all those
feet cloistered at the rim. We can't dig in

and it's murder keeping up.
A sparrow bites its marvellous luck.
The rat leans back. Dire clouds
greyly serve the puce trees west.
The city is astonishingly with us
and we're gunning for it.

What's true of things declines here:
an ordinary memoir of rage and rent,
the tuning paradise no radio can
attend to. Everyone regains
the trust of new management.
We keep walking though the cracks.

Oh, the Day

Christmas Eve, 2008

*'It never happened. Nothing ever happened. Even while it was
happening, it wasn't happening. It didn't matter. It was of no
interest.'*

HAROLD PINTER

The little ones are here for you. No birds
are mithering our squared-off sons. Ruined,
they're so alike. Their sexual minds. Words
leaking in the love home. The shunned
gathered in breakable corners beneath
wire decorations with a nice gift stunned
in this smashing place, out on the last wreath
of the citadel. Can we be bothered?
Except for some mild catastrophe in
that attributable weather: no rain,
no light in the spine of the train again?
No greed, no special dark to plead again?
It's killing me, I know I'd love to know,
King Elsewhere, where the news is dying now.

Afterwards

Inarticulate, suited-up, tie off,
hearing the engineering in ghost-thin
blond air. High white glass, the crib, that train
and grey December ice – remember, love?
The tiny cars all shoaled and shocked like fish
in Visitors' Parking, some still steaming
several storeys down. We were perfected.
Aisles of sea-borne faces, disinfected
therapeutic surf and scurf, not meaning
anything but meaning, or a taut wish
for autocratic healing. Our satchel
of promise pinched up, peeing on me
while I held him. His warm inadmissible smell
a tale of sweet polish and sour laundry.

Apollo at Celaenae

Fireworks of the afternoon. Our sky serge,
our lake taupe. The birds were bright upheavals.
Blood music banged in the lyre frame. Had I been

stripped clean in this local challenge? We were at it:
the wager that would scrape my ears from justice
and he had scudded in to listen.

Gorgeous, bristling, hysterical,
he grew in the gold layers of our meeting,
inside one core of music we could kill.

Fingers split on the strings. His sterile face
raged above my hair and tethered mental weather.
The gods' surfaces form a terror from our living space.

He leaned over the wreckers' map of me
to work things out again. My brothers wept
and beat their chests and gnawed out the dead sap

in the reeds. Would I always hang there like a ham,
a little sack of me below? And then that booming insect noon,
the redress of the sun. I was beside myself.

Denuded, I looked for the truth. Was it wrong
that we compared our powers? I hear nothing of it now,
yet all his song is staked on this. That's him all over.

On Great Cities

Afterwards M. sloped back to the esplanade
and decided restitution was twelve minutes' worth of cake.

He paraded November leaflessness.
Every lover was just a market for fish,

here was the proof
in the foreign city bakeries.

M. considered the foggy and intimate birds.
This maths drew new streets with autumn rain.

M. knew Time's Elastic Virtue
was all horsehair skirts. The final altercation

made the night a bruise. Imagine the paraphernalia
of a southern room, Palladian grandeur,

looking out over tin roofs
and all their moon-sloping winter pity.

Boys' Town

Clanging by, most patios are squalid tips pouring into lawns
of carburettors, broken baths and bogs, or leaking
pigeon houses, mossy, skeletal. The bricked-up space yawns
past with its noose of hawking kids, each red estate leaching

out their dreams with piles of squat architecture, canals and dogs.
Is this tableau meant for our sweaty Pennine journey? At gable ends,
seventies' graffiti lists the names of dads and granddads: Suggs
and Bez, Pez and Spud, the sniffing gangs who make amends

in B wing as their cage swung shut on race and loyalty
and broken knives. In these rushing archipelagos of broken bleary
Escorts and Sierras, a wintry pub displays its tarry
roof, glinting with defenestrated urban grey utility,

all of it idly monitored, and somehow happy if crappy. Somehow,
it is indistinguishable: there's the surgery (Methadone on Wednesday)
and steamy chippy, too. This methodical morning is a short ride, elbow
to elbow, hearing the stations as our thin society blows its wages, gobby

and reprieved, while the buses come to take commuters home.
The bypass has left a few suits to congregate by iron work and riveting:
gas towers, viaducts, then bookies, it's like some fifties' English poem
that guards its lines like queues of men, first sorting, then departing.

Guest Starring

for Tim Turnbull

When I look back on those dossier-rich years, the brown packages
and latex cheeks, jet-fuming plans over arrogant sand, the dark cages
of Lubyanka, the high-kicking generalissimos in Colombia,
Mafia-hosted hoe-downs and all that Cold War paraphernalia,

what I never got was Willy: the gibbon with the giant neck.
What was it with the silent treatment, Jim? Was he a total wreck?
But then, what has the ass-whupping, Commie-smashing whole farrago
got to do with *our* America? I'm still in two minds about the show.

Did you ever fancy that each repetitious script
was just some pretext for the counter-counter culture? A crypt-
ic stab at hawkish new imperialism? Anyway, the seventh season
sorted all the Sam Browne-belted Slavs. I guess we always won.

Unmasked or *Frenchified*, the whole thing trimmed and canned
like that. Cinnamon's objectified ass. Rollin's sleight of hand.
Barney sweating over dials and knobs. Who thought it would outlast
the KGB, the Stasi and the rest, with such an over-earnest cast?

I have this dream of elevator shafts, tunnels, drain pipes, heights;
misdirected collapsing that ruptures into fights.
You know, I never would have left but for some extra's crappy joke:
some lives are like a burning fuse, but yours is just a puff of smoke.

Bukowskis

for Roddy

UPTOWN

O man, I get up in your shitty shit
we're in it, baby, let me tell you now how it is
I can't take your goddamn face, you are a window on the dirt
I look out from the 4th floor up East 25th and see the dirty sun
I see the pimps and I know I eat you
I eat you and fly with my bellyful over the dirt
Even the dirt is dirt, I eat you, I eat women
The dirty women downstairs, the dirty women upstairs
I eat the dirt and I know while the music played
We loved it, loved it out into the middle of the dirt
That's it, you said, *that's where it happens, there,* and you point
and I look out at the old Lincolns sliding past Izzy and his shoes,
sliding past Evo's and Cazelli's,
I see the dirt and I eat it and the music kept playing,
O yeah, out into the dirt the dirt the dirt.

MIDTOWN

Drunk as turds this great iron night
interfering with skunk dreams in daylight
as the city's pipes and peanuts sink their sugar years
    through Leonard's
some way off 65th and we're hiding this hair piece,
see, heading down to Columbus for the meat show on the M,
free-wheeling with Big Eddie and Gloria and Peach
soaked past caring working the orange toupee in my hands
between the ferrying crew, Eddie cheering on like *Easy easy easy, Bud*
loafing and fleeing past the rich *Madams*, the hot cops,
the saturated pork night, this *perfection*, we're in it,
rocketing a little in some sheltered shit heap horseplay
and the bottles, the bones, loose in our grip like
some crappy life act, leaning a little with this little wig,
our endeavours are arduous, you said, and Eddie,
the city lights were sepulchres, were *sepulchres.*

Drilling down empty by Ruby Tuesday's
I'm ruining my eyesight for a cab on 7th
looking for the kind way out
to Fat Annie's and
the lime back wash
of vodka eats me as I stand,
I'm turning like this,
my robe is trailed out like this,
"Hank," I say, *"Hank, you're scaring the wreckage."*
I keep rinsing off the dim scabs
each night is blame's blame again
no tamer for the Alien Mite Dust Officer
on his mental home visits
making in and making off,
he'd lead me here and hold my hand
and whisper, *"Hank,"* he'd say,
"Hank, keep walking there,
all the way to La Quinta,"
and he'd always be there to meet me
somewhere on W 32nd St
taking a pee in his plaid slacks
turning for a second to watch me wink back
just
like
this.

The Naming Convention

The vinyl chairs are empty. Each wears
an arse print, like a ram's head, fading.

The canteen fills with the musk of lamb.
Music falls around us like a suit of ash.

The ninth presentation suddenly begins
with a heart singing to its daylight corpse.

The muddy congregation also sings
like macaques in the brilliant canopy.

Our mouths are tunnels into this auditorium.
Our eyes are watches from Changi airport.

Each speech opens with gold tigers
and pink lakes; a sunset of yellow spiders.

The klaxon yawns its head off
suddenly reciting honoraria to the night staff.

The corridors fill with gartered youths.
We fail at a wall of doors, slamming them

this way and that, banging them shut
at the start of our naming convention.

Everyone applauds. Above each exit, a sign shows
IMPEDIMENTA, glowing like a green smile.

We begin waltzing, corkscrewing ribbons
in decaying light. News has spread

of the congress of Ernesto and Christina,
splayed out in the server room,

polishing the lino with their tireless love play.
We imagine the moisture in red

tributaries, those interlacing greasy limbs,
their salty ears, their tidal gums, their tight teeth.

Unlit Minor Fog

for Peter Daniels

In our procession to the ends
of the cardboard apartment
where the hat stands
are wrists of ice,
our hopes fall due.

Only modern horizons lift their
frozen wakes from larder to larder,
our purpose, squashed up,
opening and closing
on a whiff of scum,

nothing is protected.
Years append the mortuary light
and the foreign songs
wheeze through all
these frozen infanticides.

Peas are the eggs of ice –
we live on in
burgundy shadows
in the roadless movie.
What could have brought

us here? Imagining
the world will thaw,
that we can save the dead
in their orange coffins
and melt the chicken news.

Austerity TV

In austerity TV, the debutantes are dead.
A crackling white point recedes on the screen
like a bombardier's view of approaching miseries.

Before the shut down, we would stand for the anthem,
as the screen's haze made us the bitter subject.
TVs have the wrong curtains in them, laundered in a fish eye night.

Yesterday's parents will make each stripy broadcast
wrestle with Edwardian troupes, or run committees
in chintz and beer theatres, quite a saga.

England will now resume its summer strikes and flies.
Everything is very large with beige skin,
or immoderately concrete, or Egyptian.

It takes an age to heat up your TV
though west of the colourless union,
there's nothing on.

We're bored of all those T55s parked in every square
and watch the scissor men prepare immaculate borders of souls.
Most TVs end up perched on a bedsit wardrobe

overlooking breadless queues in The North.
I suppose the gardeners of the free world
could ditch their sinister maintenance hobbies

and fly through The Box to where god's robots come,
or the Aquarian earth loves us even more in kaftans,
though we're hitting everyone with fresh war.

In the end, everyone stays in for corset dramas,
beastly food and wrestling. And soon the tin-topped land
will start to fly its couples south and east

where they become authentic in sombreros.
On candid islands, they unpeel like fish,
'repeats' dressed up in somewhere nearly Spain.

Willow

Under its November arms, its silly arms,
the small discretion each arm makes
and the incidental chamber
and trunk full of black fly, nothing harms
the tart core, and its wet chassis shakes
the whole winter, and I am the bare child

that wants nothing to love or to touch.
I run to it naked in the fog. Our house sinks south.
What are you risking, ashamed, adulterated?
What is collapsing in your colourless progress?
Such a paradise, then: a mouth inside a mouth
inside a tree, where the false world waited.

The Publisher's Desk

from a photograph taken at the Faber office on Russell Square in 1965

It's where that rectilinear haze of late Victorian
brick shows its glyph of drainpipes in the January sun.
Woeful curtains pulled aside the post-war
burn down and lost intentions. No one pulls together.
But everything is neat inside the office. The beetles
of the phones nearly drop off the desk.
A polished chair shows no dimpled sign of usage
and it's pushed back as if he merely stepped out
to fetch that new rejection slip from Val or sort a hat.
The right-hand drawer pokes out its brass drop handle,
perhaps from grabbing a Parker or an inch of foolscap?
I like the wire in-trays, too, emphatically stood on
four white balls like a mail room cage from 1963 –
harbouring its debt to Sputnik 1 – the red threat's
ace design feature now part of our Western road map,
collapsing into wicker staves or dog-filled heady space.
Marvellous. Yet why *two* phones? We'll never know.
The seasonal list proofs shout their tiny haven
of the future to the ceiling in Egyptian slab serif.
The blotter's doodle free the way you encounter
your napkin before some decent nosh in Bertorelli's,
but no one's settling down to something nice.
Someone austere lowers from a frame squirming
with reflections – though who cares now that
things have coalesced and ended.
                              Later, the Board
will make a note of the fiscal arrangements,
perhaps a collar will be loosened or rib scratched

beneath a dark serge waistcoat. Someone may recollect the old sod's capers, no one will believe him, and with such absent penned diadems, nothing suitable will be said and the minutes will be signed.

Cropping

I

Dear crows, I don't mind
that there's nothing left to chew
in the wild banter.

II

Our days were mushroom
fat, loyal and dark. We knew
every rotten truth.

III

In those blood thin years
we came to see the mirror
inside our losses.

IV

So the wheat fields breathe
and our car fills with evening's
taupe, *miles of it*, crushed.

All Our Yesterdays

All our children are informants.
Today, new birds grope in the cabinet,
the cake stands writhe in time.

Grandmother's war albums
float in the hairy basin. We turn on the taps
needlessly repeating all these endings.

Beyond the tiny door, no one's limbs
shake loose. There is a luminous
Watteau pierrot beneath which we

discover a pile of bedpans, mattresses,
single shoes with smart red ribbons.
A vertiginous tongue is glued on top.

We buy some of everything.
We jump to it.
Then they wheel in the lead baths.

Ending Up

When I die, I'd like that committee to meet me,
intent on breaking up my sagging heap.
My mind will be running on empty,
parading its leafless isthmus.
No one should remember me.
All my attempts will be armpits.
In fact, I'd like my giant works to fly inside me,
postcards to the gods, except for
the godless boulevards. And possibly
there could be beatings for my incontinent
disgrace: an army of insouciant
beauticians with maracas, to bounce me out
to a breathless brick heaven.

And you, all of you, can simply let me go now,
into the dusty cassette I have left for the occasion,
repeating endlessly the cracking story
where the man in the empty body dawns
inside this bruise of no loveliness, inside
the spanners of memory, parched,
hammered if he could find the gin,
got out early and might now begin.

On the Small Print

Today, we read the small print after closing.
The shutters clattered with continual thieves.
This was perfect, we agreed.
Today, we read the small print
and congenially noted, among the almond trees,
that no one wished to die. In the small print
it said we must yearn for our general apostasy
and flames were, like pigeon shirts, no use.
Soon, Amelia handed round the torching papers
with a little pepper, and considered, secretly and still,
the imprecations of the worm.

Whose the savage skin? she asked.
Where would the animals fit?
How was this procedure less yellow than the Thames?
Later, the wind burned all its horsehair off.
The night put out its melodies in sacks.
We fingered through the footnotes and
loathed our mothers' waste, for today
we read the small print and everything adjusted
to minute angles in the frost.

We came to the bit about the great sad doors
and bartered this box of small grey boots for it.
Its opening smoke concealed all the edges,
yet this was all to end, the small print said,
when we stepped forth into an idle bridge
beside the winter foam. Even the rooks
would look into this gulping night and weep.

Lost Brother

I know you could never turn aside from me,
an ear at my closed ear, the beer breath around us then,
forks of sound our arms abated in, the brothers with
nothing on in hot weather. I just had to leave you, yet
listen, I can tell that our love for this old place
takes its neutral phantoms, its bare tongue, and leaves us
both the vertiginous *O* that no one now could cure.

I like it that you live in me still, an ember, a loyal child –
when you stretch to speak in the russet tangles of the stem
you are withheld in my mental coral, a blood speech
we shall always be arranged in, the brothers,
under foreign scarves and future loss, behind, arrayed,
I see your sightless tiny hands, that peculiar half-kiss,
as my life draws in to your permanent night.

From the Frontline

Once your eyes have adjusted to the burning,
scan through the racing battalions,
that mouth, idle elbows, then tilt your head like this
to observe an arranging sea of grit. You can sense

the singing or crying, crying or singing,
where it is this high-minded sort of commotion
all day. Anyway, no one wings it
in the compound. We're poverty in motion.

How we ended up here is funny, like a shiny
belly or bare flank, or it could be just that ash-
coloured, hose-damp concrete there.
Every child distorts the man, and man the cash.

Look at it raining down – sordid, localised love
beside electric couples filming, or fleeing,
the gift. It is an entirely live feed as we learn scripture
from the telly. Someone says, *'Nomads in waiting,'*

as we become scintillating, free in the debris.
Don't catch life out, then, and watch the traffic.
Now you know when the slap-up meals fall out
of those sacks, we'll be taking home our pick

of your bomb-retiring heroes, day and night,
night and day, those clean-cut silent flags filled with
hamburger heaven, warm under props. Later, we'll
be zooming or seething through that dream

up dislocated arterial routes, shaky gorgons
in the *Zone*. Together again, we are a modern fog,
the idea of the better dead, immortalised grey
eyes above subtitled, totally-idealised dialogue.

No one adheres to the precise terms any more.
The streets shiver like widows this afternoon of very
large government. We'll ape out the speeches
of the ape. Our country is his artery.

Damaged Enamel

A whelk-coloured fissure there,
submerged in tidy, slightly pissy, water.
It looks almost sandy square-on
and the bath's near-white enamel
seems grainy to touch.
Nearly split, but not leaking,
and in the minor surface error
that you rub your toe on, to test it,
dull parades of infancy coalesce
inside years and years
of weatherless sloshing.
Put your head under and taste
the deaf interior, then feel your balls
move in the cold skins of the water.
Everything is the bright surface
of being eight and, aloft, remote,
remoter now, the summer winces
at its loss, the wet futures scurry
under the bathroom heat lamp
with its scouring corona and useless menace
and a hundred dinners forgettably
arrange their albums elsewhere.
The fissure carries on for twenty years,
thirty, forty, waiting for the soft parent
to return and glance over the renal
empty sadness in the bathroom, the way
every bathroom is an inner absence
we wash ourselves from, out of, denying

and recovering in equal measure
all the torrid dreams of cash and power.
They rise like steam from each white hulk.

Fat Diaries

Let me confess from the start
that everyone sinks on Fat Street.
Everyone is gorging in the nameless district.
I stop to cram the crackers, fill the cracks.
Fat is my new you. My ankles blacken.
I can't fit my shoes.
This day moon is a wok.

I become astrology and rubber blood.
I fly past all the frying stars. It's heaven.
Everything's a joke and the joke is me.
This street here, where no one cries,
where no one strikes a match, this street
is the mirror I am blind inside.

I cannot see myself. The bigger I get,
the more I hide. I belong here.
Mr Universe in the road show of absentees.
I am a great disease.
The end that comes in a heavy bed.
All the shelves are stacking up for me.

I'm in the happy room, I can't bend any more,
my life is this food show warping
a birth attempt, I'm breeding me, unwrapping all
the gold liveries to stare into an ungovernable night:
the great, grease empire. It's soaking in,
this new knowledge. I think everyone will join.

A Northern Icarus

It's where we clamp our feathers on,
stroke the stove pipes, clatter off in droves.
The tatty gingham terrace shines
with sunbeds like a furnace mouth
and there is shed life in Leylandii shade:
a town arse-deep in crated sleep.

Then all this painful crockery in the night.
Tameside's shaved municipal lawns.
Everything is pure Victorian gothic bent
beneath the glue pot moon.
But here we feel that sickening air lift
and come off all Gagarin.

O red lord of the chimney tops!
The sickle-shaped rupture of ideas!
Our stinking night rain loosens and there's
coal smoke under buttocks.
Yesterday's life-maps shriek with glee
and Droylsden's cemetery suits are free.

So what you have of us is entirely
an explanation in shawls. The blown crows
explain their looks and I was about
to sing around Ashton's tar-life looming.
A history of meat. This naked flight
that is the last of middle-aged arithmetic.

Down at Jim's Place

Kettle's Yard house, Cambridge

Jim's house wears its journey like a bed.
His rugs are thin. His windows misted up
with looking out too much.
I like the cacti on his sills, their little
dusty lives all settled there like eggs.
In that room of sketched heads
upstairs, we piled our minds like
wreaths, imagining Ezra's portrait pouting,
as we are shoved out some place else in time.

It made me think about Gran's place
one silent Payne's Grey Sunday
in Torpoint, her solemn budgie
piercing the septum of that Cornish
interior (*mordant* for mother) –
and no boats for Wallis. Yet here,
devoid of light's narratives we look
shifty in this afternoon of neighbourly
objects. This tall-backed chair
sings its cliff-song: clacking
Presbyterian beach dreck and gulls.

Imagine the swanky evenings
of high music, where an interlude
of flared pants and big hair sauntered
through the love-ins, herded and gushing,
while beauty was this chantry,
secular and white, like a voyage east.
The sum of things is an infanticide,
we live inside it, like warders ageing,

all shored up and in between,
creaking figures with no advent
of coronal ocean at our misspent end,
the paint now dry on our lives.

A Short History
of the Manchester Riots

In Chichester Road, I lost my teeth in 1981,
on the pavement of a social studies website not begun,
in cream and orange ciné 8 where gangs were surging
and everyone wore big hair and pixie boots.

It was *opéra bouffe* outside Loreto college
where the needy queued in second-hand serge.
Observe the brass-knuckled uppercut in slo-mo
and watch me kiss each shining node just so.

No hanky for my running mouth, the zygomatic bone
depressed and nose gone for a Burton,
I travelled off imagining a month of tubes and soup
from that place of the Sisters of the Blessed Virgin Mary

to Manchester Royal Infirmary,
and waited for the goats in white between two boys in blue
like it was Orgreave or Maltby and the lines were drawn.
But that was all to come. A few years on, the Tory dream

would cut a of swathe of diffidence across the pews,
wearing Westminster's finest ketchup and Swords of Truth,
while far-off Hulme was history: we knew our ruin had begun.
In Chichester Road, I lost my teeth in 1981,

with a face like Mickey Rourke after the umpteenth face lift,
or bulging like a Stan Lee über-villain with my crones.
I learned that culture meant six months of dentistry
and justice was the sordid life of bones.

The Victorian Amusement

James Berry, hangman (1852–1913)

We live inside its tin frame like peg dolls,
drinking soup, playing canasta. We watch the fire's ash
build like a mind. Our beds are tiny mushroom beds.
It is very neat inside the empire. We button collars
beside the painted privets and suffer mild angina
while trains scream through the milkless hours.

Each morning, we watch the banisters twist
further round our lifestyle. Outside: old horse manoeuvres,
fastidious ironwork peeling. Suddenly, we move upstairs
away from a brass sun. Could such small terraces
become our infanticide? The orange hoses perishing?
The drawing room is hung with virtue like a shawl.

Of course, we bury everyone in the coal yard.
Later, they will return with cats and weather:
painted bodies, chatting stiffly: *Hullo!*
We love your thimbles! We yelp and count them home
in the silted scullery. Moths fly from their hats
into the metal India of the years.

All these imaginable lives wind down.
We will always be there. No door will shut properly.
The thin streets will begin their massive decay
and soot walls judder back to show the sudden gallows,
familiar in foundry light. *The masked story of perfection!*
And a child's eye. And the penny going in.

Coast

Cromer. Published as the Act Directs August 17th 1779.

Everything ends up in closures of light:
boiling dreams, bear sagas, rickety Dutch wanderers

bereft of green rags in a parky summer sunset
upbraided with the 18th century's planetary chatter,

the clever void untold and a packed coach
muddled with weeping turning its sweet flanks

back to Norwich. Welcome to fish fables,
net-kept wives in flint-corbelled soot, witch-driven

interior terrors giving way to rearing cloudscapes
each forming articulations of herring,

a town that comes and goes in the worryless evenings,
eventually singing a sea, an iron sea, with

the total fist of thought, and all-comers know the tidal
sagging that reduces each to leisure here.

Take the aristocracy in the marsh-ridden market
sloughing salt attendance with their next of kin,

alternating horizons patching their eternities
with prismatic cargo. The cliffs fall in. The boats come in.

At night, we see the town's escapades and destinies
in a tiny fantail of light the lighthouse sends

and resends in dull twists, it fetches up
the brassy cumulus with a grimace. Even moon wrecks.

Everything we know of it is a poverty of tunes,
shoeless wretches at the burning station,

tall gods in the general enormity of weather
and in the prison of a kiss, the lovers put together.

Motel Sentences

1. The 4 a.m. telly is offering up of its local chat show laxatives.

2. All-night screaming sexes up the siphoned city wah-wah.

3. Furniture wax, the corporate art, bequeaths its lonely love lagoons.

4. Droopy aquatics next to this nightly deliquescence of gumbo.

5. Inside the one inch, no-jump zone of filthy air: a legless pigeon.

6. The ten footsteps to the light cord intend to be elegant.

7. The shower with its wigwam of razor cuts and business news.

8. Here is the epidemiologist's mattress of gannets.

9. The full English wrestles with its perfect membrane.

10. *Eat my shit, Pagliacci, this motel's run by clowns.*

11. A soft shuffle special in the shower's fresh garland of pubes.

12. Backing into latex, we smile up at the Artex.

13. Stetsons and shoe lace ties confuse the Bolton zumba group.

Promenading

The end of pier show
pours its ragged sound upon
the unlit breakers.

THE END

Lightning Source UK Ltd.
Milton Keynes UK
UKHW010620200522
403285UK00003B/357